Adult Coloring Book

Floral Creations

Stress Relief Patterns

Judy Fisher

Publisher 2016

Floral Creations Coloring Book

©Judy Fisher

Judy Fisher has asserted her rights under the Copyright, Design and Patent Act of 1988, to be identified as the author of this work.

ISBN-13: 978-1533351838

ISBN-10: 153335183X

Designed and Illustrated by Judy Fisher

Find me on

Instagram: potsetc

Pinterest: pinterest.com/potsetc/

Coloring Ideas

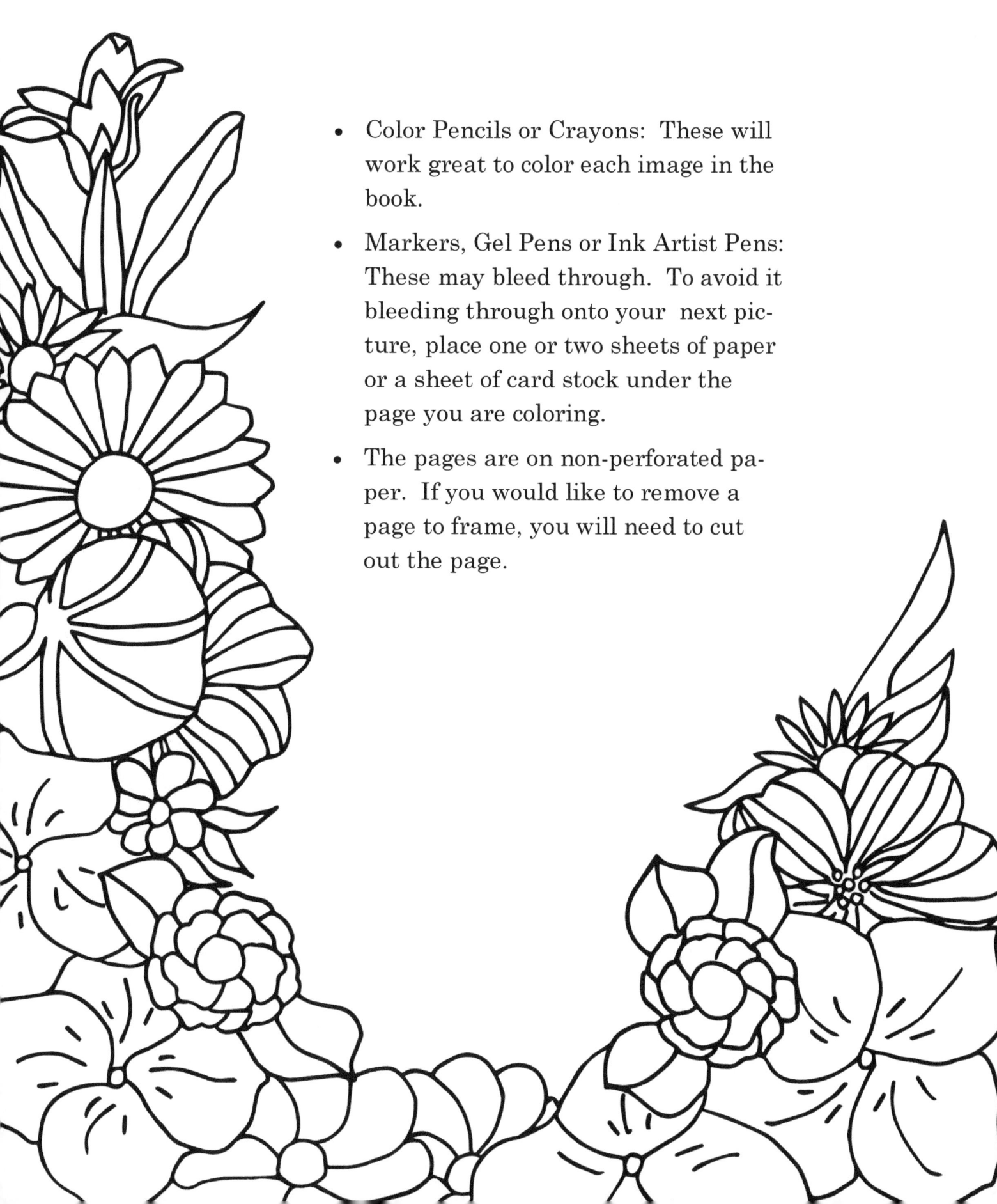

- Color Pencils or Crayons: These will work great to color each image in the book.

- Markers, Gel Pens or Ink Artist Pens: These may bleed through. To avoid it bleeding through onto your next picture, place one or two sheets of paper or a sheet of card stock under the page you are coloring.

- The pages are on non-perforated paper. If you would like to remove a page to frame, you will need to cut out the page.

Every once in a while we need to stop and admire the flowers. There are so many colors and hues to enjoy. My personal favorite is the Texas Bluebonnet. Because of this, you will find more than one of these floral designs within.

This coloring book allows you to appreciate the floral designs while adding your own touch of color. Find a relaxing place, choose your coloring medium and compose something new.

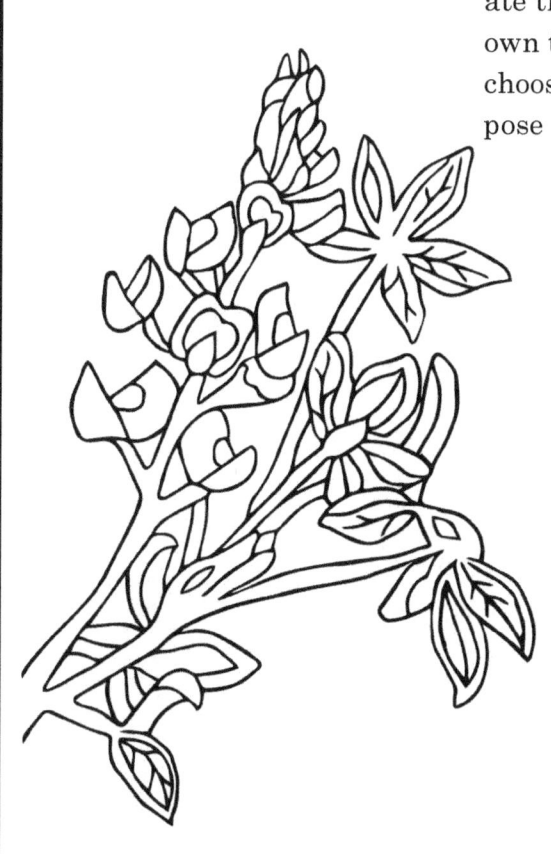

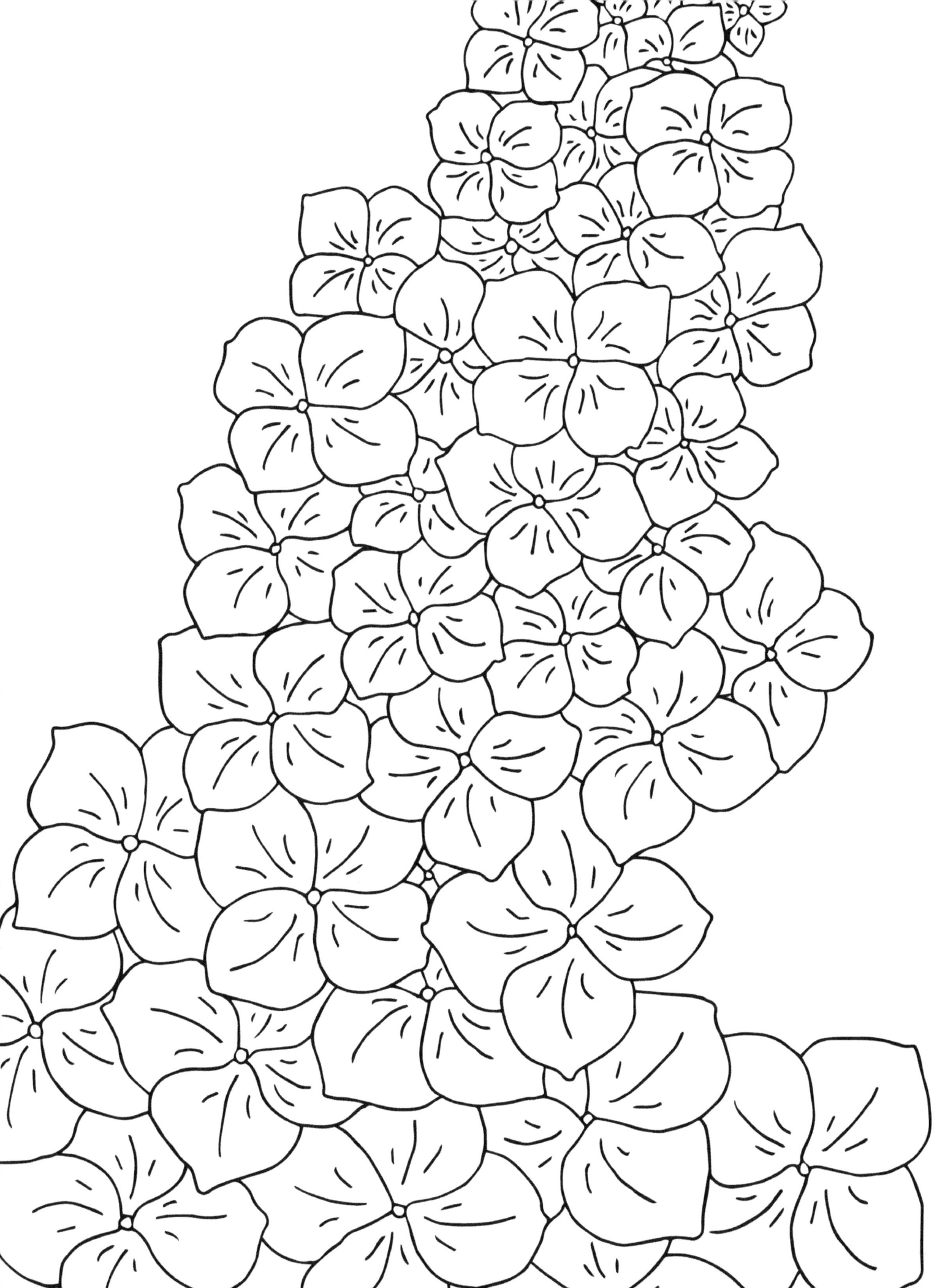

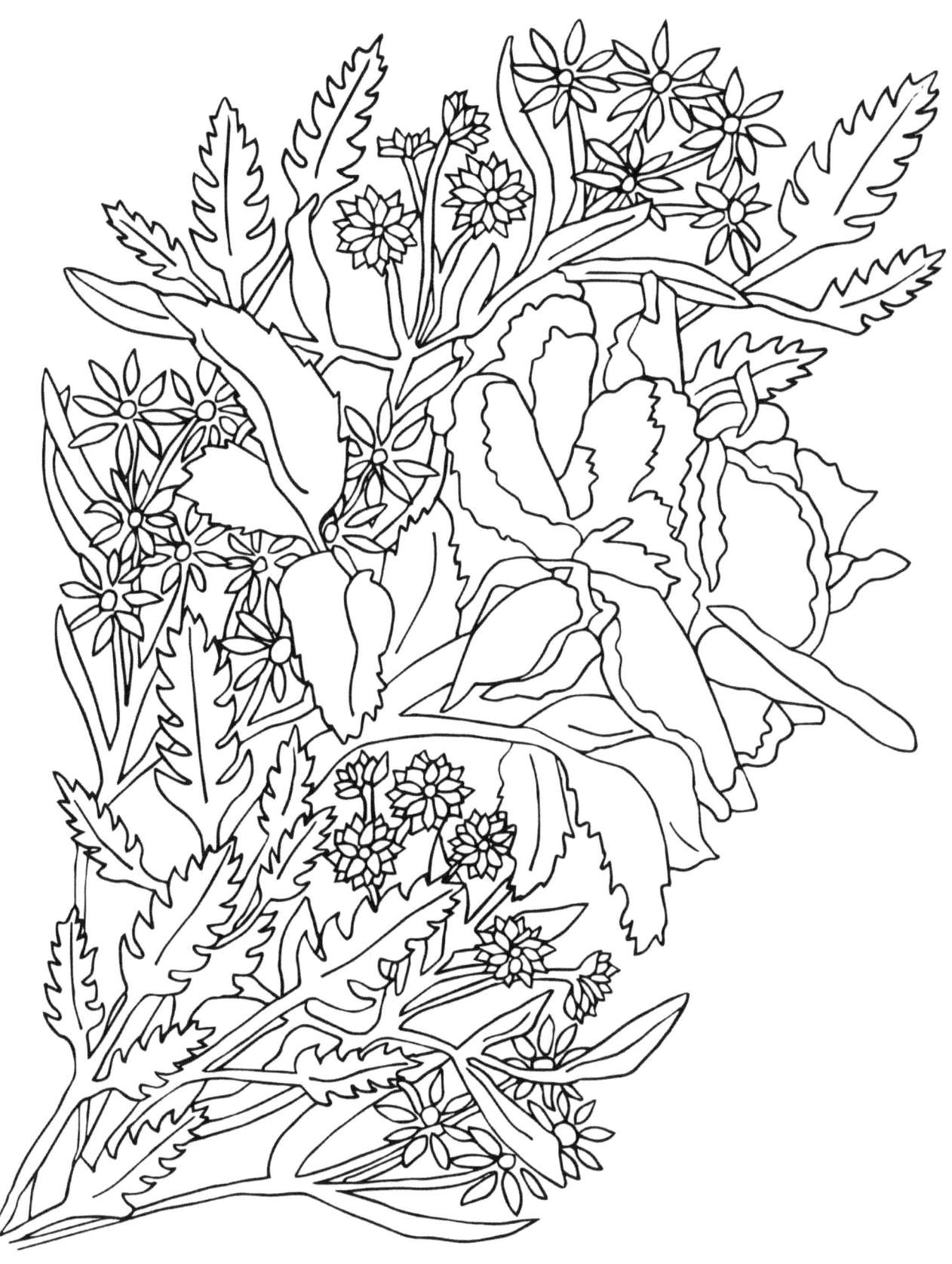

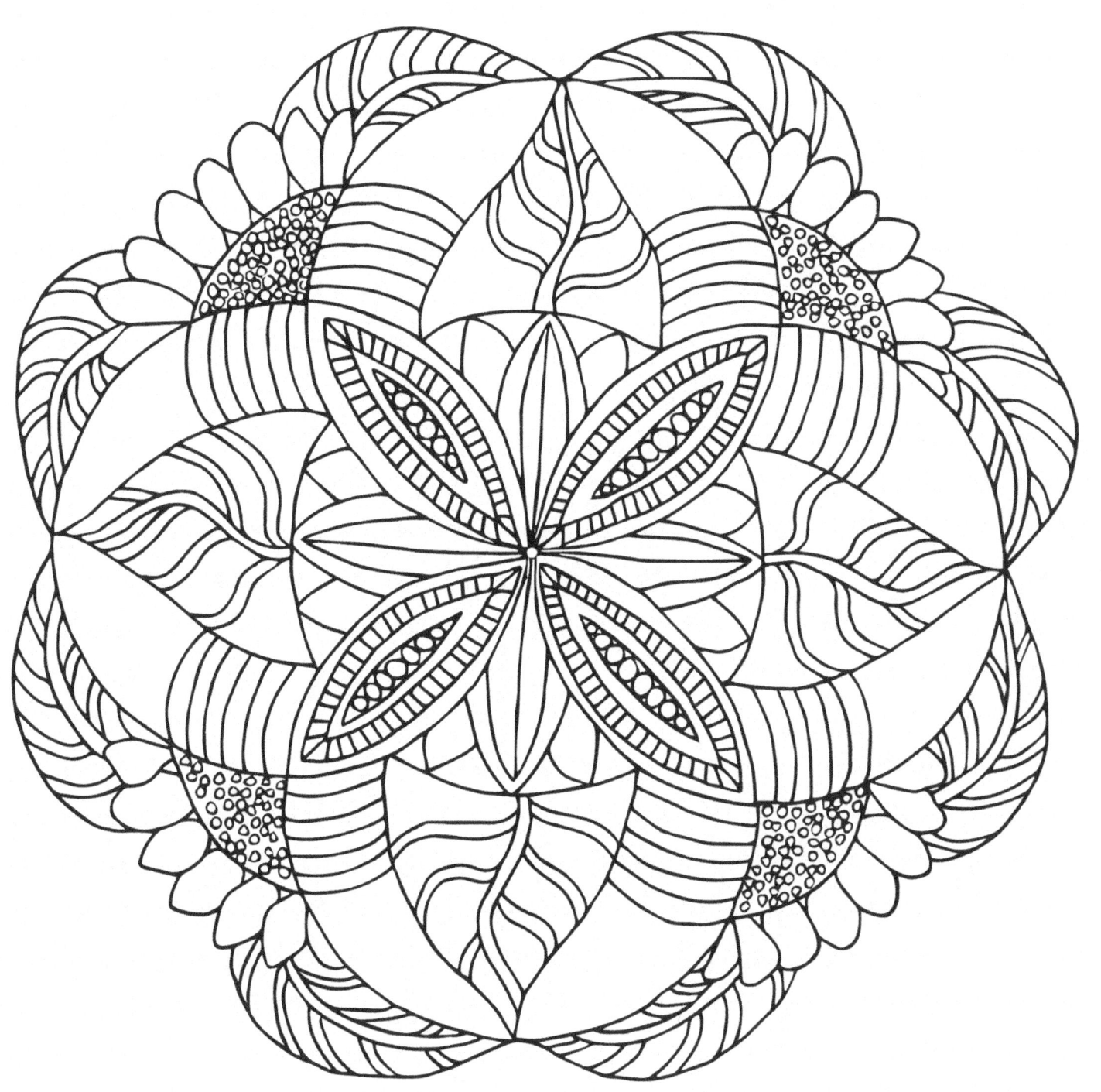

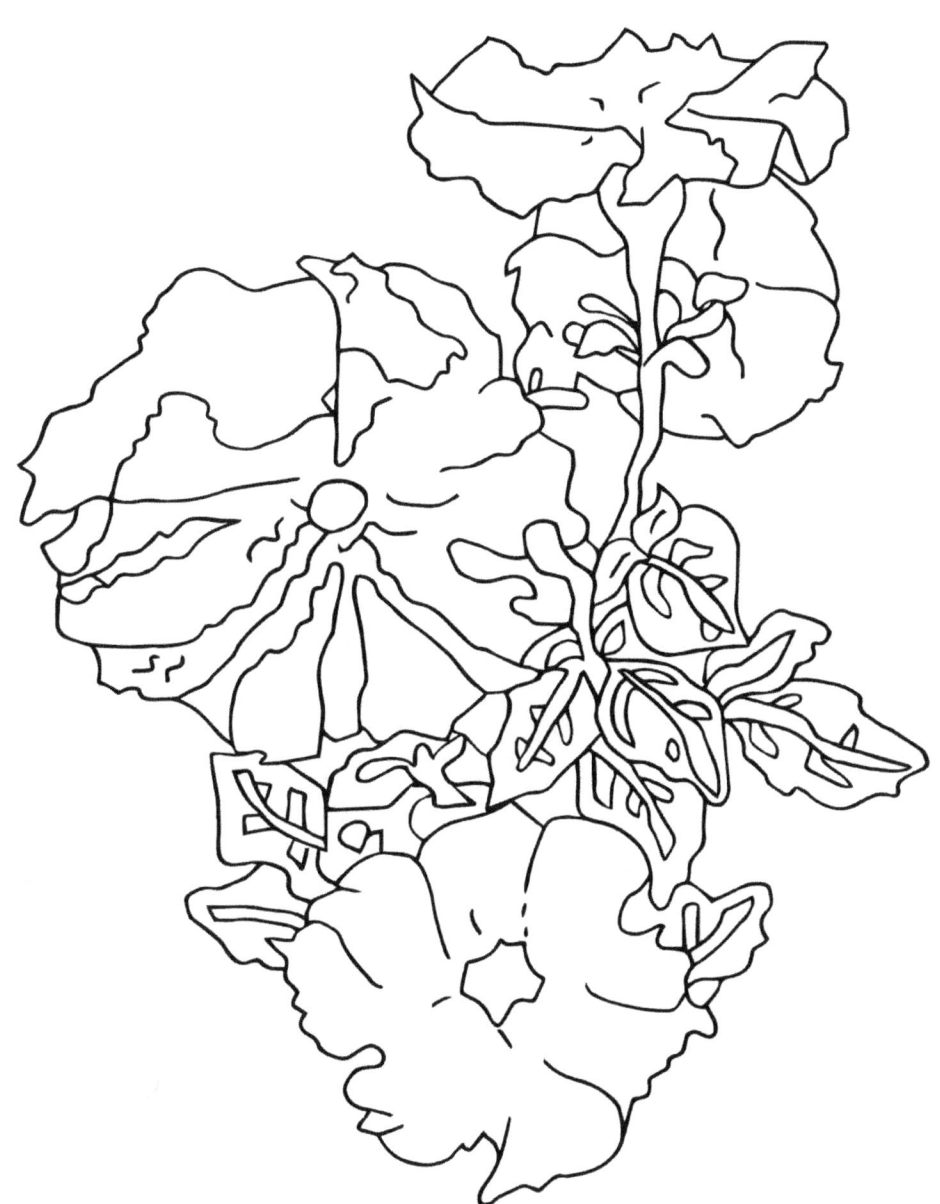

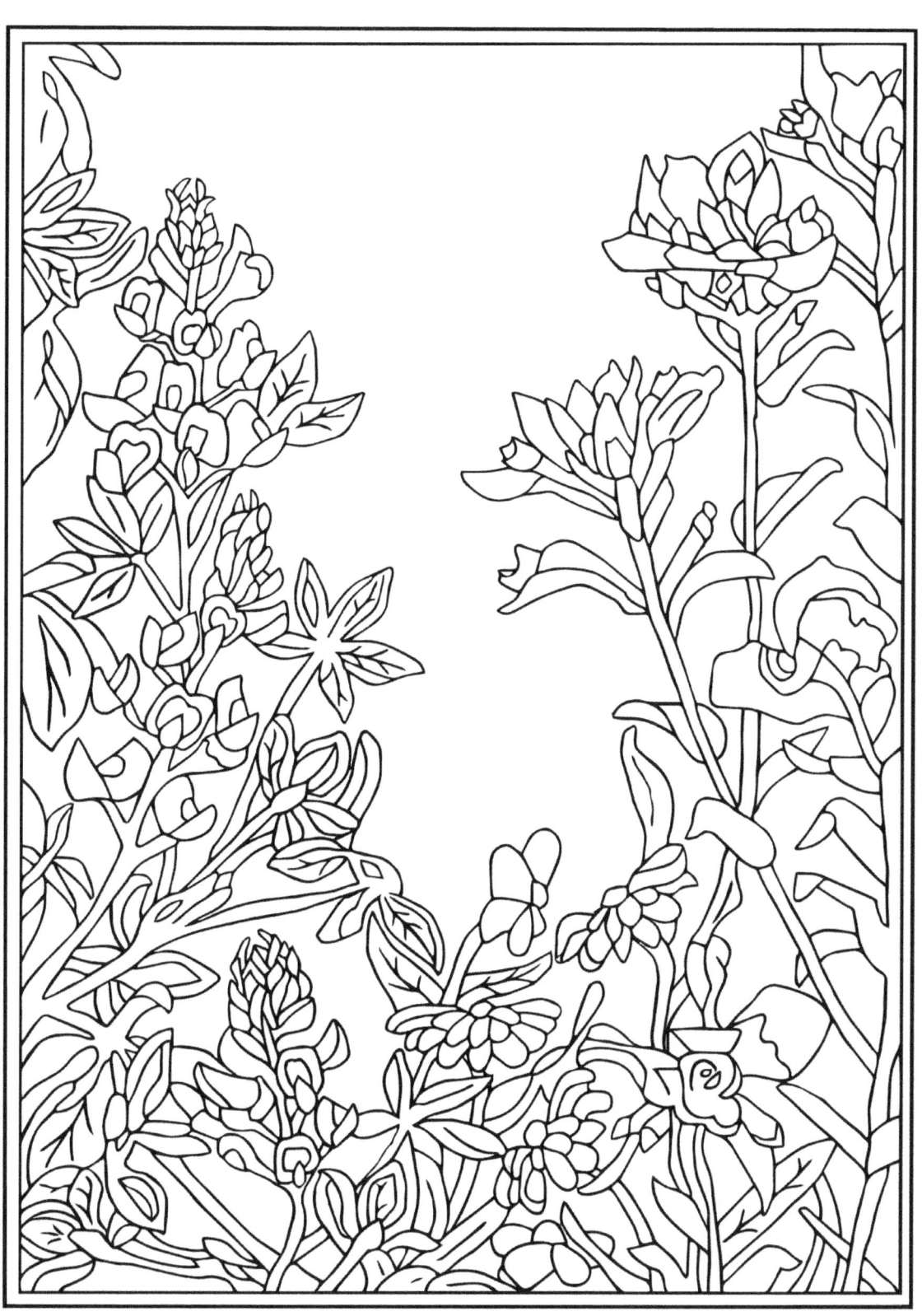

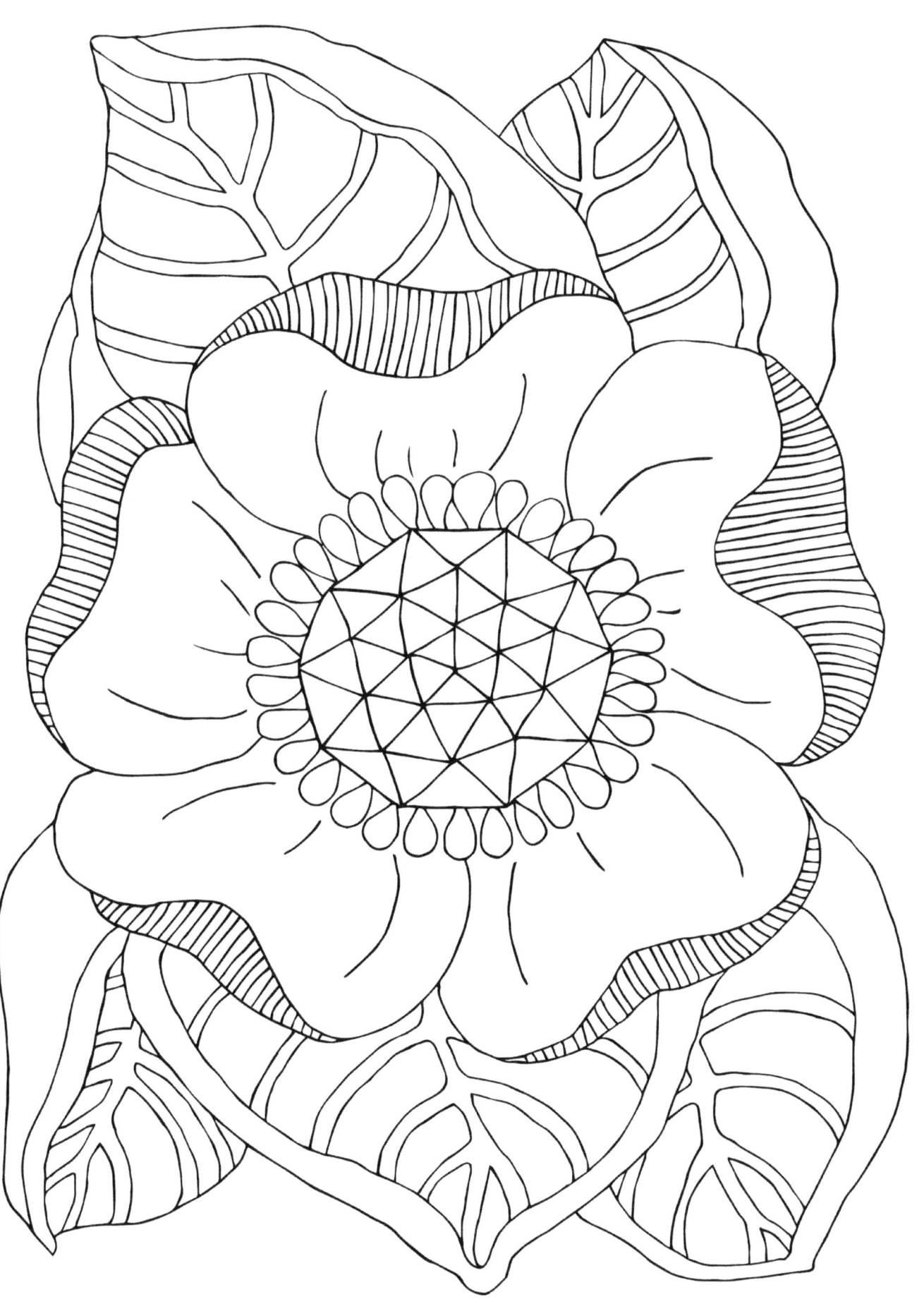

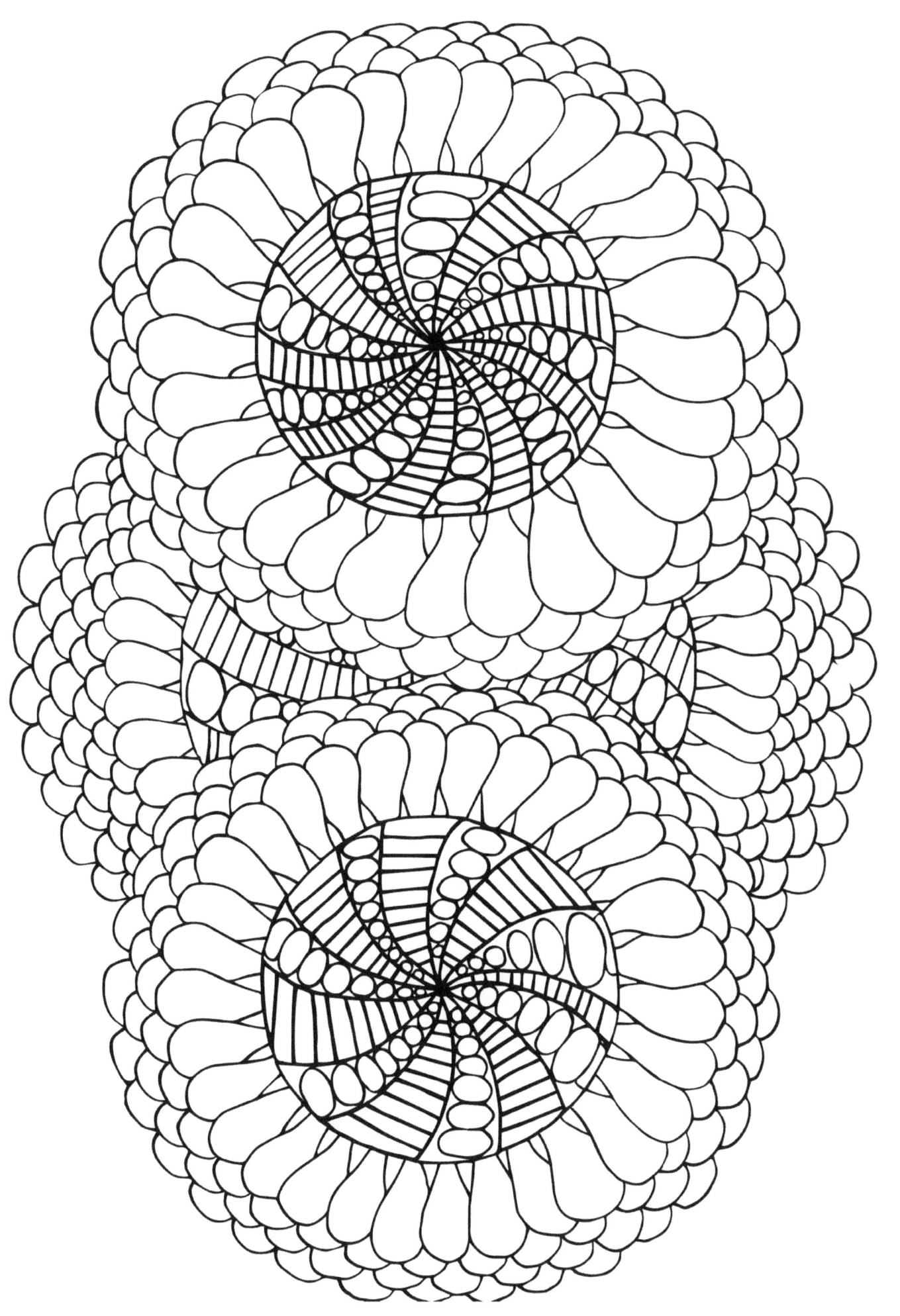

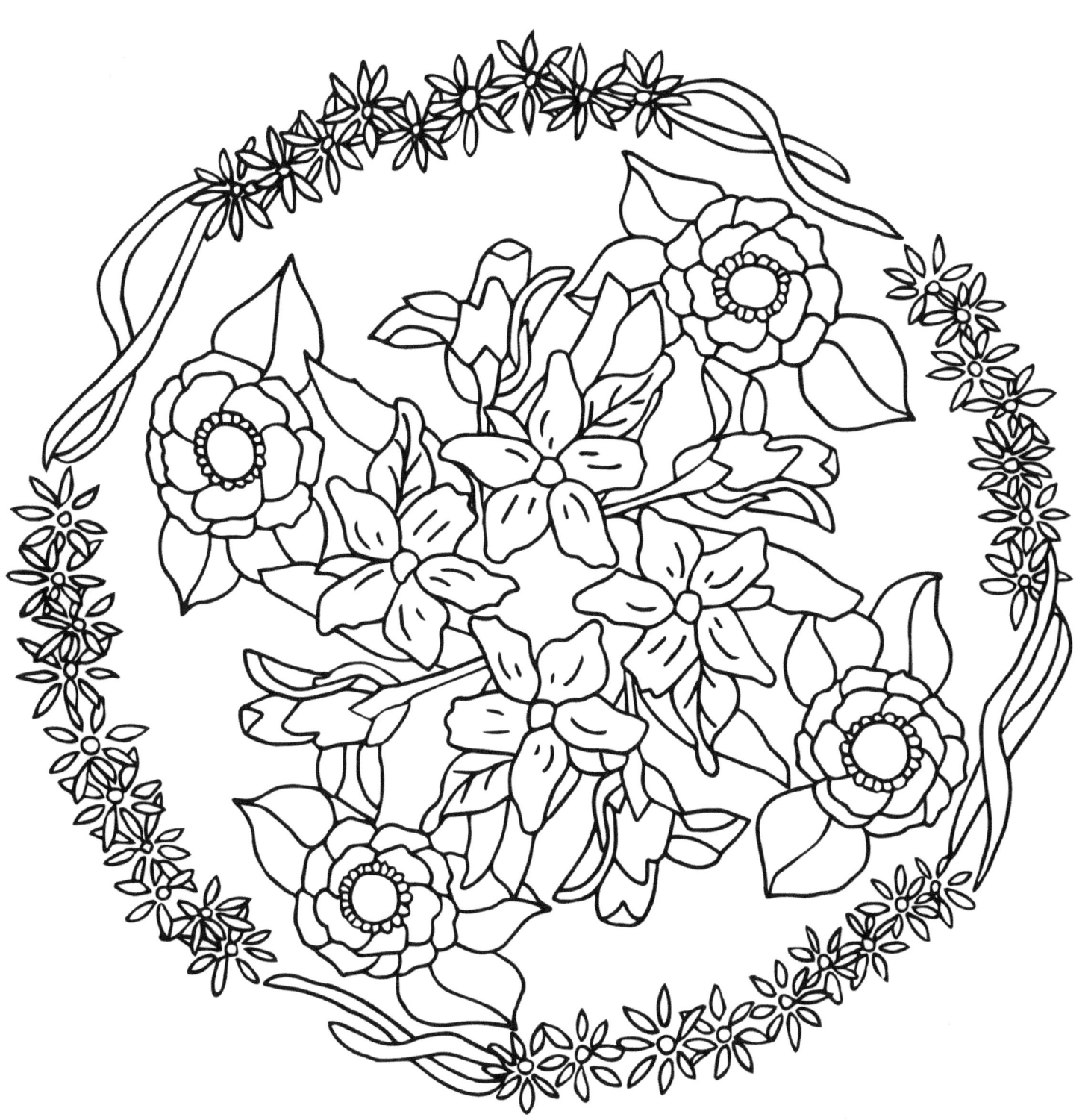

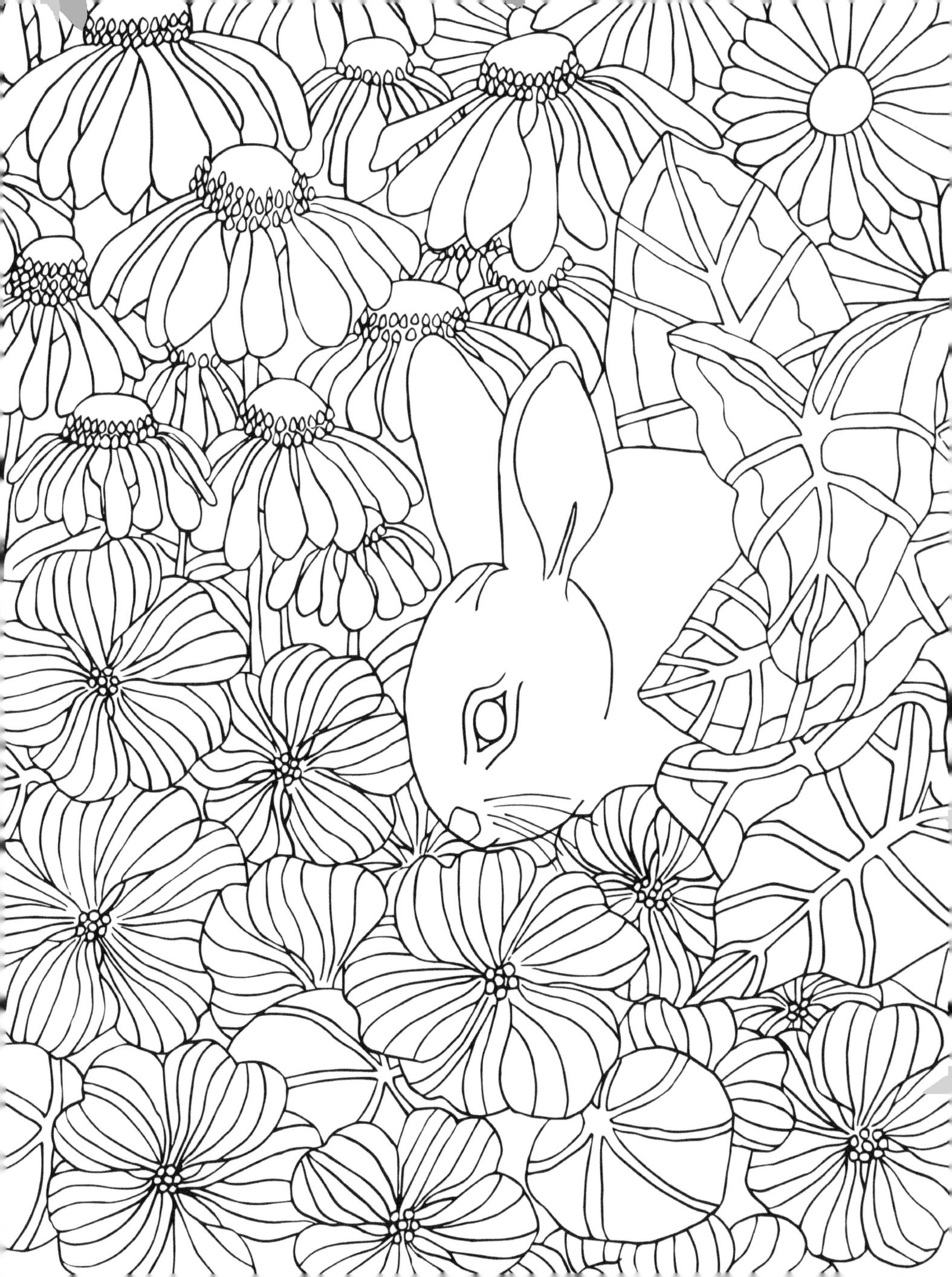

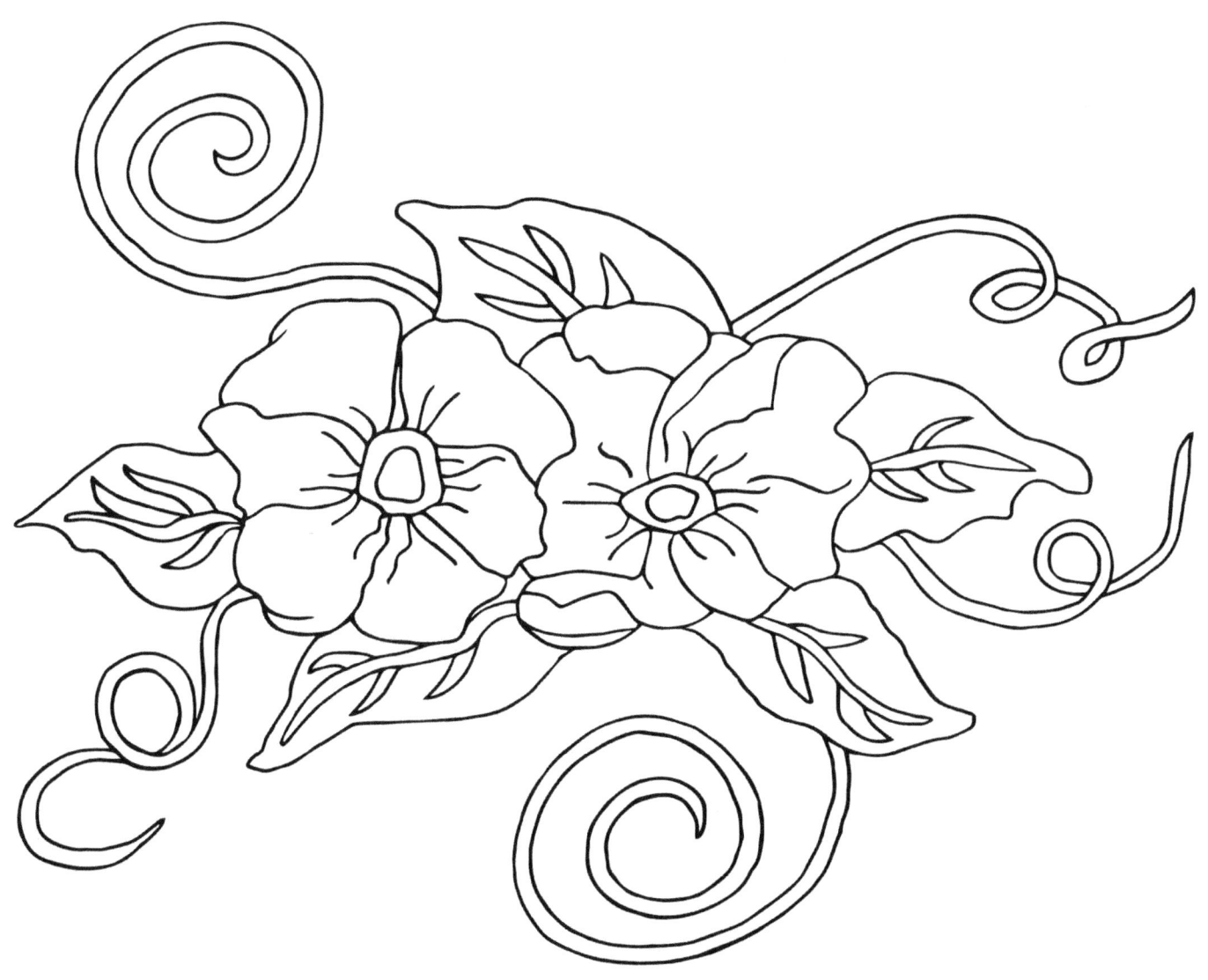

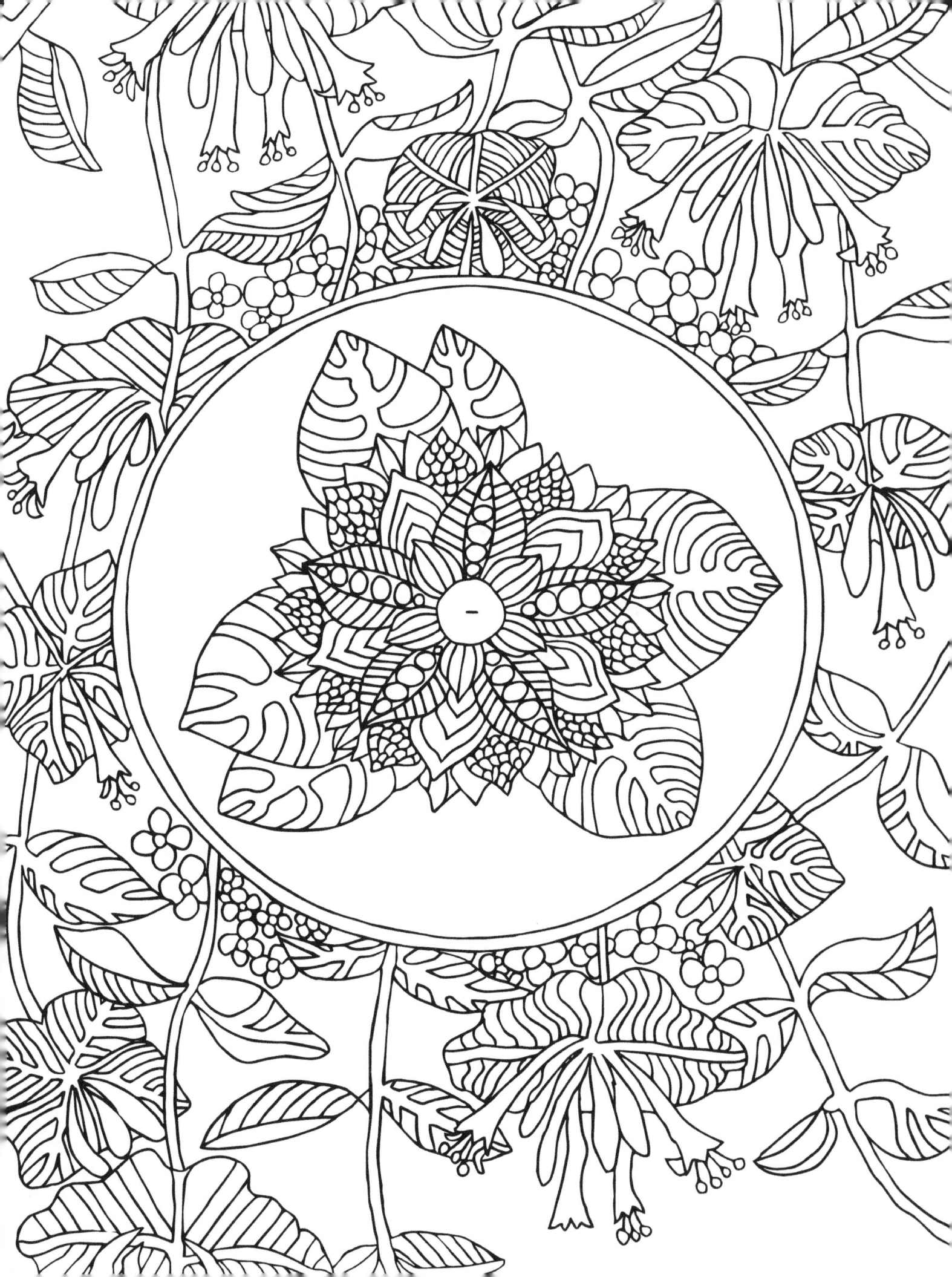

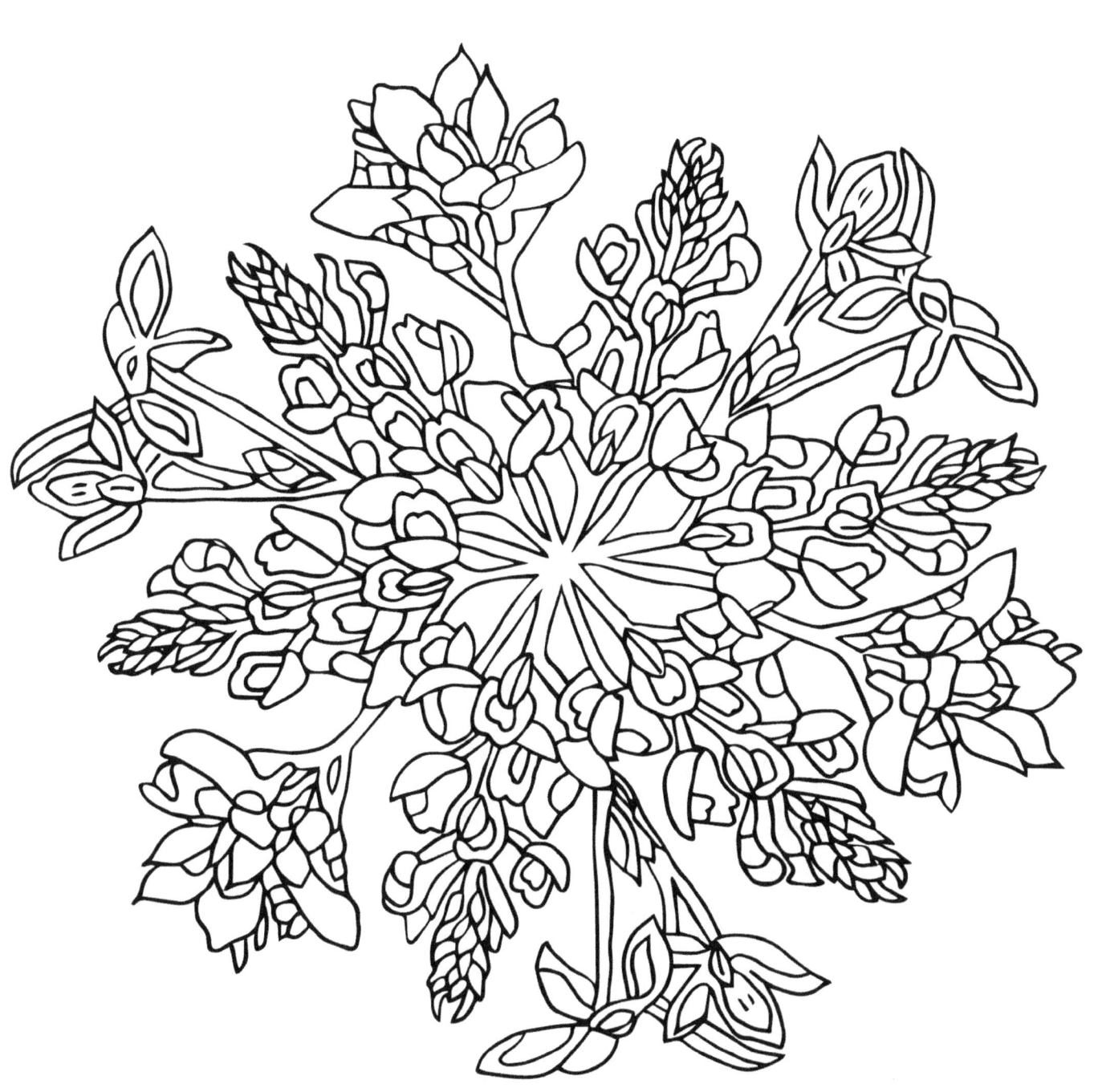

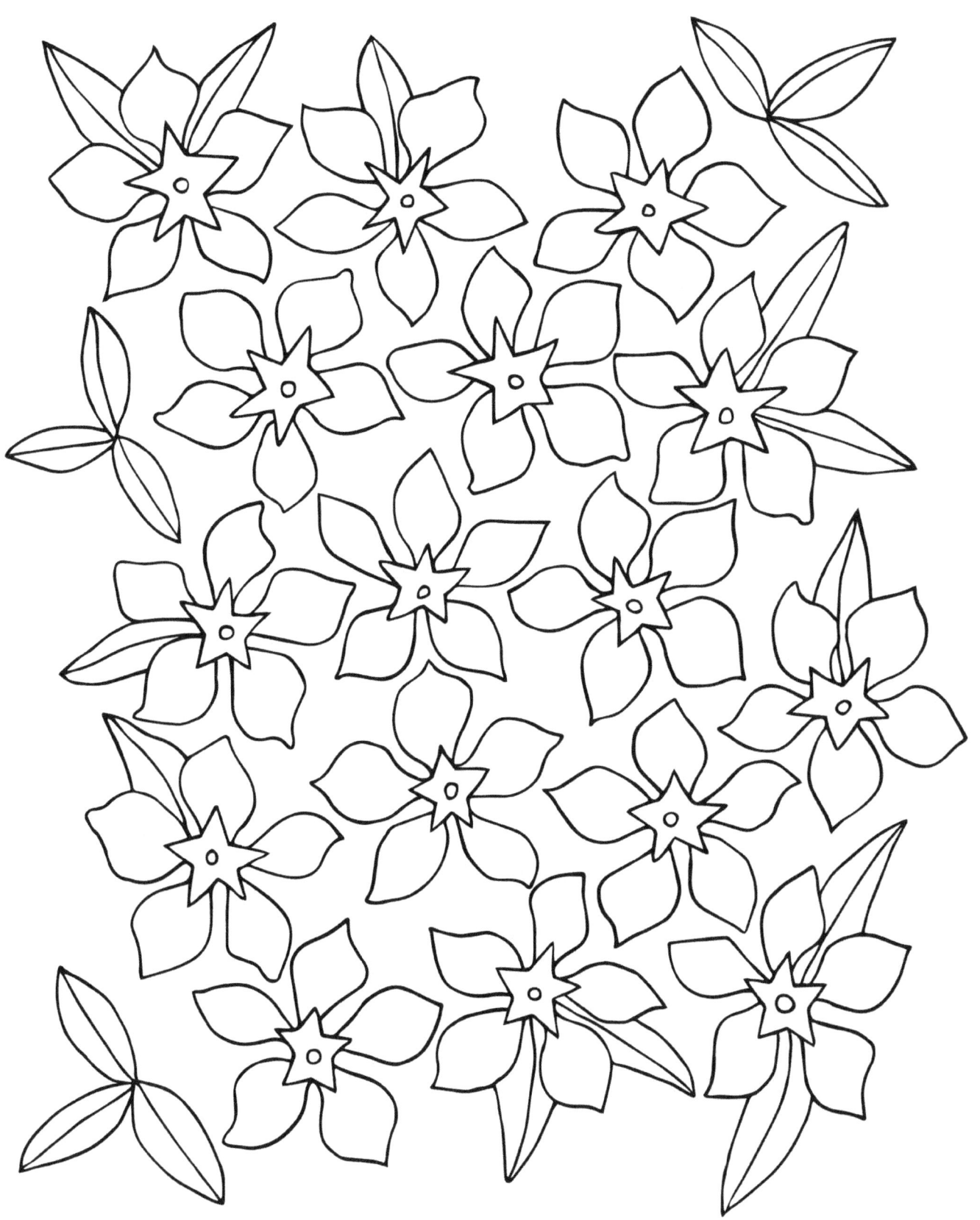

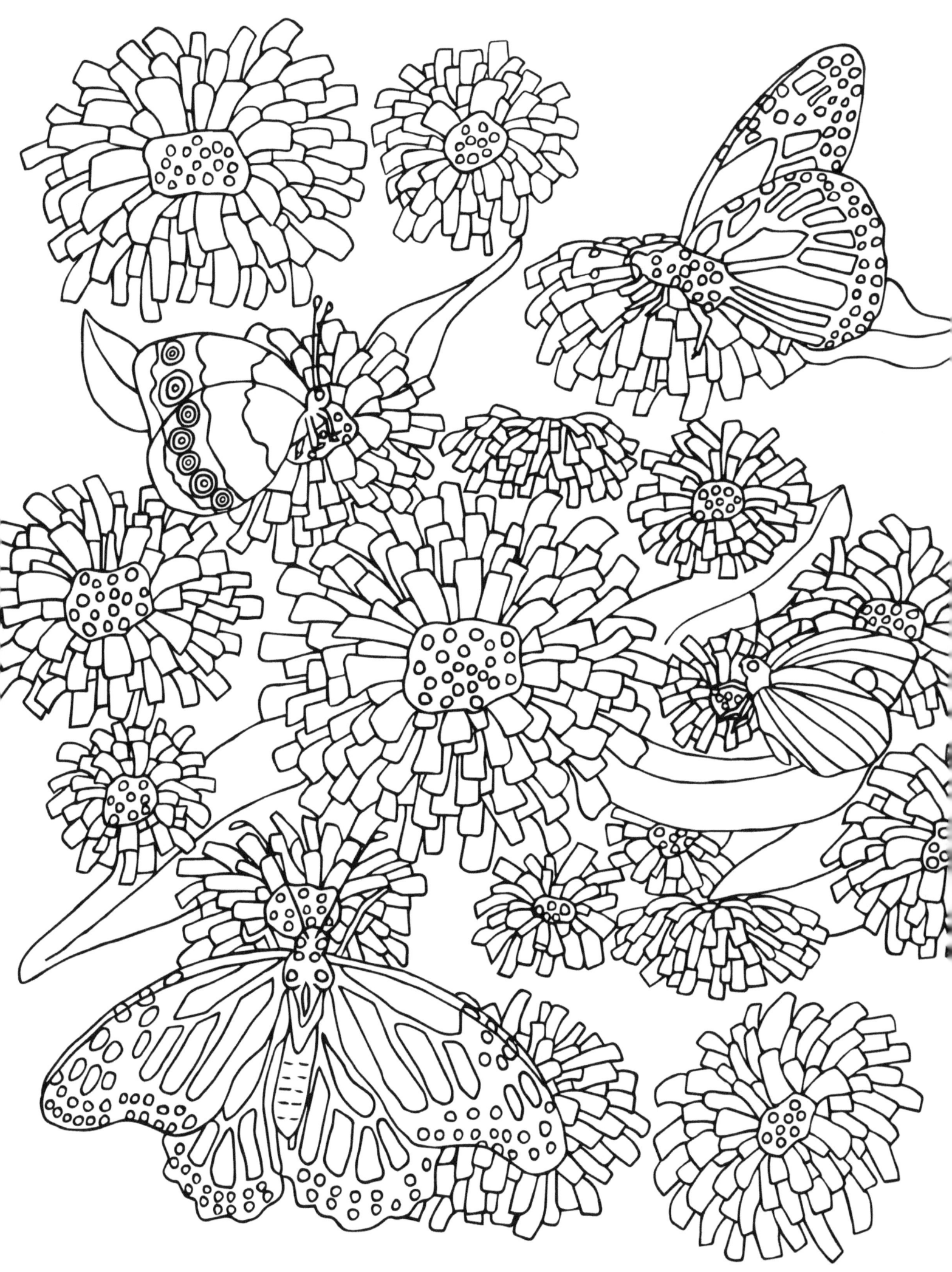

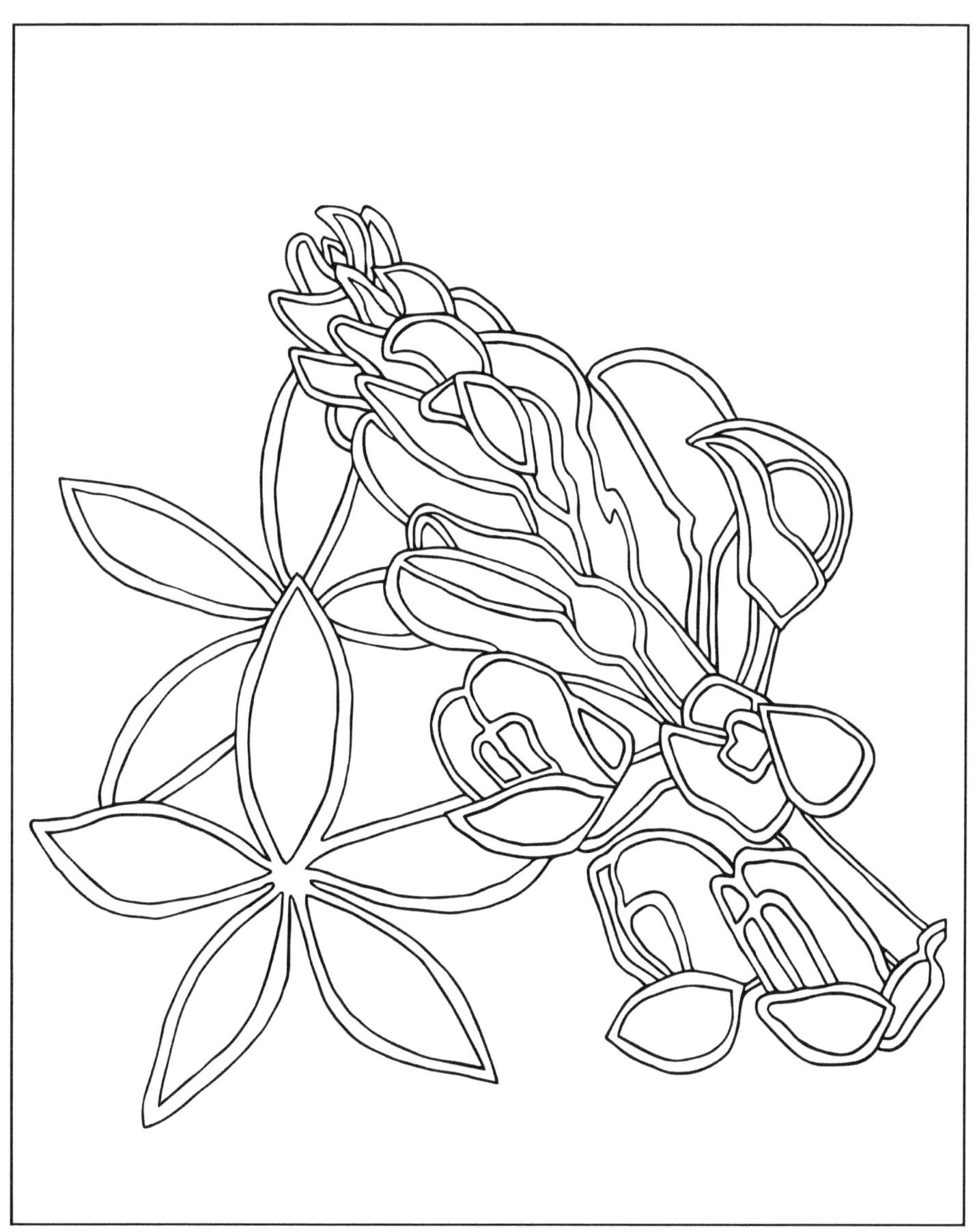

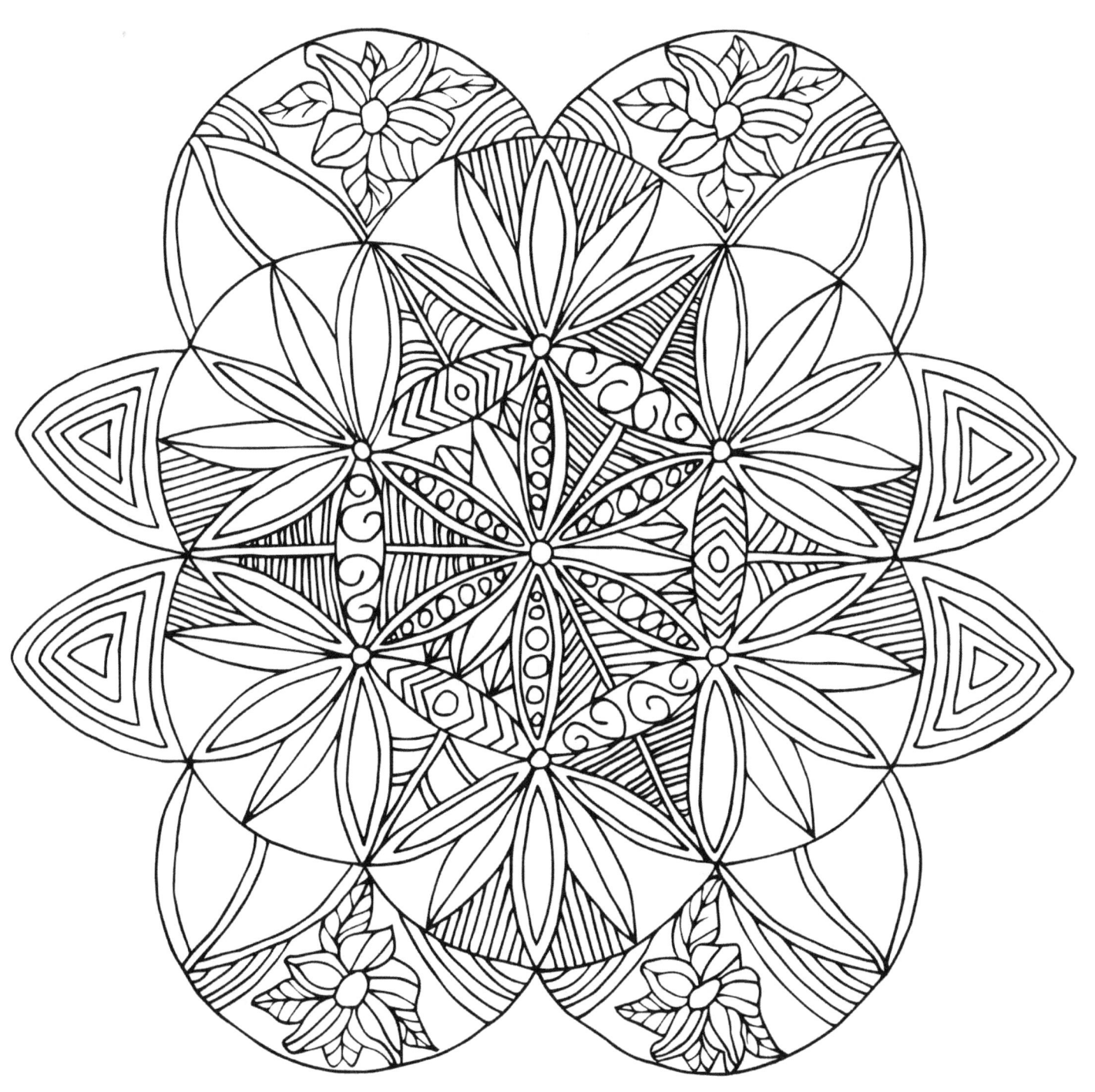

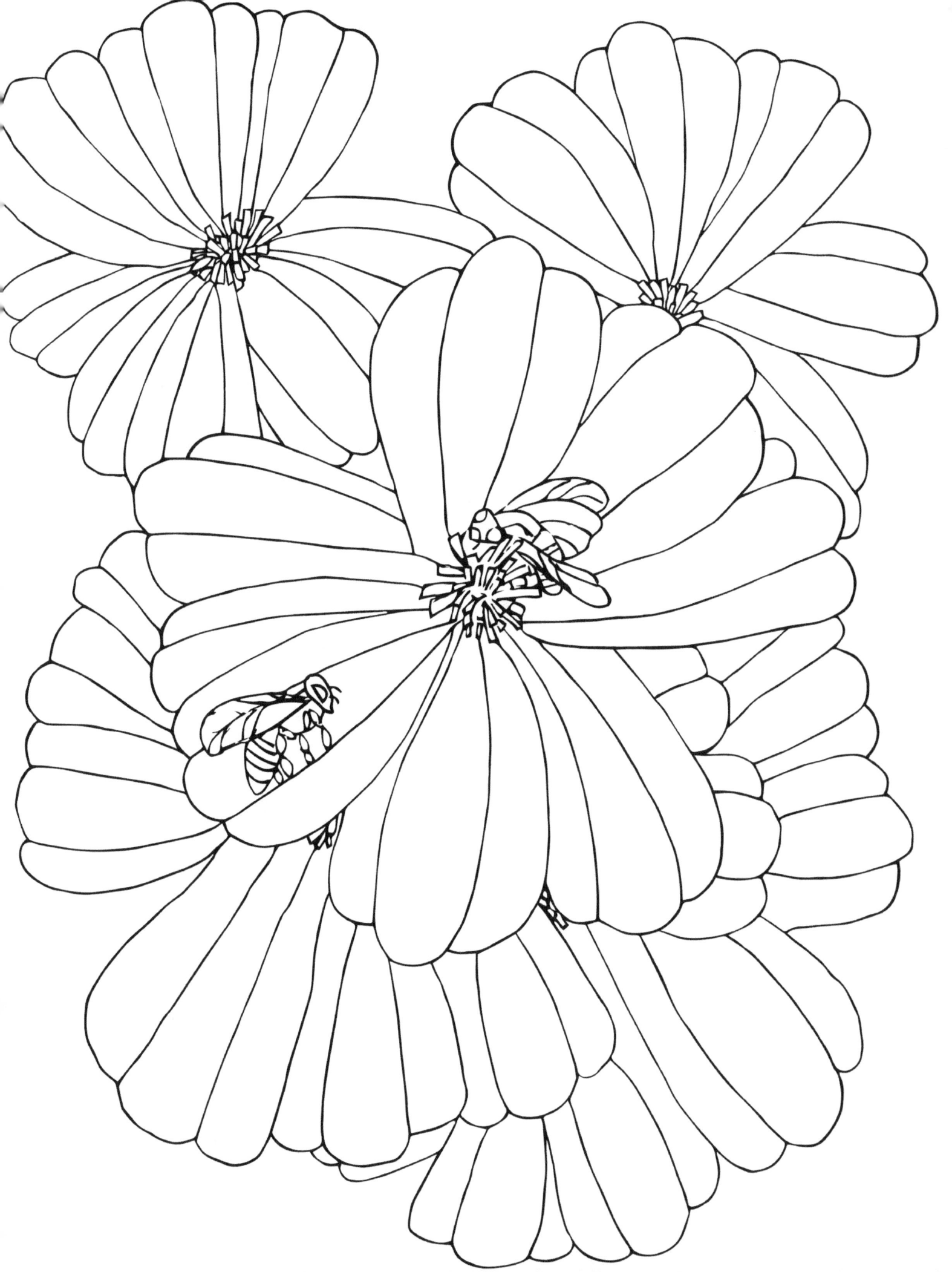

I would love to see your creations!

Load your pictures to instagram and
tag me @potsetc.